350

D1399810

YOU

should be interested in —

TURTLES
of the United States & Canada

BY

CLIFFORD H. POPE

illustrated with 99 photographs

TROPICAL FISH
and Their Care

BY

NORBERT LEDERER

*with illustrations by W. Hammersley Southwick
and Diana H. Furth*

Foreword by C. H. Curran, D.Sc.

These are Borzoi Books, published by

ALFRED · A · KNOPF

LOOK AT LIFE!

Look at Life!

A Collection of the Nature Photographs of

LYNWOOD M. CHACE

New York & London

ALFRED·A·KNOPF

1940

EDITOR'S INTRODUCTION

~~~~~~

This book is the fruit of a boy's hobby that became a man's life work. Lynwood M. Chace was a lad on an old New England farm in Swansea in Massachusetts. There he was born, and there in the morning years of his life he gave himself up to the bright world about him. What he learned to see then, in the pools and among the grasses, was to become the subject of art and study filling his later years. No thought of worldly success, however, spoiled that period of his Nature love; it was all a long idyl of curiosity.

Stevenson has called curiosity one of the chief talismans by which we win our way through life. Certain it is that a boy's curiosity is a spark of some of the divinest fire in mankind. In those keen, careless years it burns very clear; it may all too easily be extinguished as the years roll over a youth with their weight of problems and burdens and their grind of the commonplace. But in the luckier, that spark takes hold, burns brighter, becomes a steady flame that illuminates the purpose of the man.

Of these Lynwood Chace was one. He remembers the young years now with a relish heightened by the knowledge that all that happy loafing was in reality a steady march toward his present stand. The old farm was a world to explore, and he wanted none wider. For he was gifted with an acute eye. Let the grass rustle or the branches stir, and the boy was still as a fox in his tracks, watching. So long he stood motionless, observing the gray squirrel circle an oak bole, that he came to feel himself a fox; the thrill of the predator ran through him. Nothing of the hunter, however, seems to have marred his boyish sympathies with wild life. With a sharp eye he marked down the duck paddling in vulnerable innocence on Swansea pond, the heron stalking elegantly along the brook bank. But they were safe with him. One more picture to store in his memory of nature scenes was all the lad wanted to bag.

But, being a boy, of course he made collections. Having an eye for beautiful pattern, he prized bird feathers, when he might obtain them without harm to the bird. If he started a grouse in a woodland thicket, down he would go on hands and knees and brave the brambles till, by careful quartering, he found the prized rufous quill. He learned bird calls, as a farm boy will, with the birds for his only teachers. He knew where was the nest of vireo and flicker, of oriole and red-winged blackbird. Patience, that stubborn virtue on which he was going to draw so heavily in his later work, grew and strengthened in him as his curiosities grew. He could lie still as any one of the shadows gathering along the lichen-grown rail fence where at evening, he knew, the whippoorwill would come again to shake the dusk with its tremulous repetitions. There is no excitement purer than that of the watcher when the wild thing comes close, close, and in a breathless moment the shutter of the mind clicks on the unforgettable memory.

To catch the population of wood and swamp and meadow in their intimate attitudes takes a perseverance of which few boys are capable. This farm lad had it. The distant pumping of the bittern teased him to go and look, go and find it. No bird call is more mysterious a summons, since it is unimaginable that a feathered throat could give forth that sound so like the blow of an axe head on a stake, combined with the sucking sound of the stake driving into soft ground. The "stake-driver," moreover, has a trick of pointing his head upward on his long snaky neck and freezing in that un-gainly pose till he is indistinguishable from the brown bush next him. But the boy who had climbed to the top of the tallest tree overhanging the meadow marked out that bush with a cunning eye, and knew it for the bit-tern it was, and heard the hollow pumping call rise from a throat he could see pulsating.

A brook ran through the farm into the woods, and a brook, for a boy, is better than an ocean. To feel the cool water lapping your bare legs and the sand ooze tickling up between your toes is so keen a delight that it remains a fresh and delicious impression in the mind of Lynwood Chace today. For the most, a man looks back on the boy he was from quite another world; if it was an unhappy childhood, he is glad he escaped out of it; more com-monly he gazes back with regret at the lad he was, remote and secure in the shining sphere of another and a different existence. But Lynwood Chace is still inhabiting the world of his boyhood. The woods, the farm, the brook are still there, and so is the same old zest. The wading boy who glimpsed a spotted turtle swimming downstream ahead of him went splashing after, stumbling over rocks, plunging his arm to the elbow to snatch his prize and stuff it in an overall pocket. Nor would Mr. Crace today hesitate to plunge into the babbling icy water if he had his heart set on the portrait of an egregiously grinning turtle.

If it is true, as the well-known affirmation has it, that a poet has died young in the breast of each of us, it is even more certain that in every boy who opens his eyes to the light there are the beginnings of a scientist. For boy curiosity, abstract, disinterested, absorbing, is the first step upon the path of science. The path has many turnings, into other fields. One of these Lynwood Chace took — a footway very little trodden, and leading into the heart of all outdoors.

It seemed, at the time, that he merely stumbled on it. He was nineteen, and the bright outlook of boyhood had been suddenly dimmed by a physical breakdown. Nor was the young man allowed the resource of work to build up his morale; his health did not permit it. Now the farm, once so complete and teeming a world for him, became a desolate and barren sort of place. Then an elder brother returned for a visit and made the casual and pregnant suggestion that Lynwood take up photography as a diversion to brighten his mood.

Not that the boy possessed a camera. He had to borrow one, a simple box affair, and he invested in one roll of film. The first pictures he took, of some robins feeding on the lawn and of a green heron on the lake's edge, are distinct in his memory — far more distinct, alas, than they appeared upon the developed print. All that he had captured of his robins and his heron, after all, were a few remote and smudgy specks upon the paper. This is the point at which you either give up, or go forward with an energy that can carry you the rest of the way. Which Lynwood Chace did is told by the collection of pictures which make up this book.

So remarkable a photograph as that of the spinnerets of a spider or the close-up of the star-nosed mole is not attained, of course, without years of experience and training. But now Mr. Chace had direction; he knew what he wanted, and, more important, he knew what he did not know and how to go about learning it. The pursuit of his new hobby in the open air having greatly improved his health, he ventured to approach a professional photographer with the offer of his services, for what they might be worth. He made no boast that they were worth any remuneration other than the experience he might pick up in the studio. On that understanding, the photographer took him on, and the boy worked eagerly, finding his way in the world of the lens.

At last, armed with new skill and a new and better camera, he set forth in the field again. Now he was able to make some nature pictures that brought him satisfaction. Not a final satisfaction, for this was a game that grew only the more interesting the more you played it. And he thought of it still as a game, a hobby. No idea of commercializing his interest had occurred to him. It was another brother who gave the young fellow a kindly push toward the direction of profit. He suggested that Lynwood's pictures might illustrate one of his own stories. But when Lynwood set forth to the city and braved the editor in his lair, it was the story that was rejected and the pictures that were eagerly bought. Editors ever since have been snapping up the camera captures of Lynwood Chace.

What characterizes these photographs is not a scrupulous scientific exactitude, for their maker does not hesitate to pose his subjects sometimes, the better to display them. Thus he has caught detail that would escape a lens focused on the creature unaware. Much ingenuity has gone to some of his achievements. The irritable darting dragonfly may be stilled by a whiff of ether, just long enough to catch with the camera the tremulous sheen of its wing. Or Mr. Chace will build a blind and lie long hours in wait for the desired subject to approach and take an unconscious pose. To photograph the interior of a bee's nest requires not only patience and ingenuity but courage as well. But hours of trial, unlimited gentleness, and an inventive audacity are all part of this photographer's equipment.

Like a thumbprint on many of the pictures is a touch of Mr. Chace's whimsy. He frankly admits to posing many of his shy little subjects, but takes the more delight in the happy effect of elfin fantasy he thus achieves. He does not claim to be, in all these photographs, an austere reporter of natural phenomena; rather has he, in some examples, created an art-form all his own. And few of us but can find a child-hearted pleasure in such pictures as that of the wide-eyed mouse peering over a moth's shoulder, or the portly toad at rest between two toadstools. This is the innocent underworld of the grasses, the pond water, the roots of the benignant oak. Here, surely, remote from unpitying mundane logic, we may enjoy the caprice of a unique imagination.

But in certain of the more remarkable photographs in this collection the accuracy of the lens transcends imagination. It becomes the eye of a veritable magician, perceiving that which is hidden from unaided human vision. The magnification of a single minute detail, like the sting of a hornet or the jaws of a katydid, does more than show us its particulars; it strikes the observer with a startling realization of how much more there is in the world all about him than meets the eye. Mr. Chace nimbly performs the function of introducer to this Lilliputian complexity. He presents us, face to face, with a tortoise or a longhorn beetle, and such is the power of his camera work that the creature positively looms at us with a verisimilitude next thing to alarming. This is not only to see the world as it is, but to get a very healthy viewpoint of our own selves, as being not so exclusively important as we fancy, but rather clumsy and myopic obstructions in the busy way of bees and ants, frogs and wood thrushes.

And Mr. Chace has an instinct for significant design. His picture of the salamander clambering with antique reptilian grace upon the unwonted loveliness of a skunk cabbage gives a hint of this talent for seeing beauty where another would pass it by in a stride. Nothing is too ugly or affrighting, by commonplace standards, for him to look deeper at it, and find its interest, its significance, perhaps a revelation of its genuine æsthetic value. The proboscis of a moth, for instance, shown under his magnification, not only ceases to have any repugnance for us, but is shown to be a thing of geometrical perfection. So too with the pearly and iridescent eggs of a slug, with the squirming half-nakedness of young skunks, the purposeful symmetry of a snake's coils.

We are all of us become purblind since the passing of clear-eyed childhood. We look, and fail to see what lies all about us, the dazzling variety, the significant detail, the patterns beautiful and strange that underlie our own gross pattern of civilization imposed upon nature. Once in a while there comes a man to show us what we are missing, sometimes with the written word, sometimes with pencil or brush, in Mr. Chace's case with the incorruptible testimony of the lens. What he has seen, we too can see, for the looking. More, what he has done is not, in some modest sense at least, wholly beyond us. The hobby of nature photography — and for Mr. Chace, although it earns him his livelihood, it remains joyously his hobby — is one beyond none of us who have our sight and the use of our fingers. It is the earnest hope of those who present this book that it may lead others into fields wherein Lynwood Chace has so happily triumphed.

THE EDITORS

I

FUR AND FOUR LEGS

This peaceful meadow is a teeming world, that on one summer day is filled with drama and mystery, beauty and horror, song and labor and battle to the death. The worm at the grass's root, the butterfly at its breezy tip, the birds flying overhead, and the mole burrowing in dark of earth below move each in its separate sphere, each to itself paramount. So we see nature as the adventure of manifold little lives that together make one great flowing Life. And with that stream we too are borne upon our mysterious voyage.

This cottontail was too young to protest at being removed from the nest to pose under a head of Queen Anne's lace. The hands that lifted him were gentle, and on the log the sunshine fell warmly on his back. Life will teach him to be less trusting.

The star-nosed mole is a fantastic example of specialization. His powerful front paws, with which he tunnels his way in the darkness of earth, are huge in proportion to his soft little body. Compensating for his nearly useless eyes, the astonishing snout is extremely sensitive, the two main blood vessels in his head going out to the very end of the hose.

The white-footed mouse is a creature of elfinland. It lives in the woods, perhaps in a bird's nest or hollow log. It loves to scamper abroad at night, when its big bright eyes are sharp on every shadow. By nature it is gentle and unsuspicious, seldom defending itself against capture, willing, even, to become a pet.

This is nature as a child longs to find it. But the young bluejays are not in fact come to call upon the squirrel. That bright cock of the youngster's eye is in astonishment to find himself upon this threshold, and the squirrel, returned home, is as puzzled by his visitors. Such little animals, however, lend themselves, in skilled hands, to the making of such fairy-tale pictures.

The raccoon may be thought of as a kind of little bear. For a home he chooses a hollow tree or cavern. The crying of the little ones when mother quits them to go hunting is absurdly like a human baby's protest at being left alone.

A nimble climber, the raccoon sometimes curls up for a nap in the nest of a hawk or crow. Or mounting to the top of a thick-foliaged tree, he may ensconce himself in comfort among the branches, unseen from below, secure for a time from the teeth of the hound dog or the steel trap.

Raccoons have an appetite for all sorts of food — berries and bugs, snakes, fish, and young birds, to say nothing of corn in the milk. They are easily domesticated and, like this greedy trio, make diverting pets.

Upon soft ground the track of the racoon is easily recognizable. Its print is long, with a narrow and distinct heel, and one might guess that a child had been running here. This raccoon child, however, has no chance to set foot on the ground; the gleam in his mother's eye is of determination not to let him get away.

Above: Squirrels make entertaining friends. They seem to have little fear of mankind, and where they are not molested will live as his neighbors. If it is not too far to jump from their treetop to your open window, they will come visiting at the offer of a few nuts, and even sit and eat these sociably in your presence.

Left: Lifted from their safe nest in the hollow tree, these gray squirrel babies, only two weeks old and blind as kittens, yet had the steadfast instinct and claws already strong and sharp enough to cling to the tree trunk, which they will be scampering up and down in a few weeks more.

Hawks and squirrels are intimate only in the wonderland of storybooks, but ingenuity created here a glimpse of that happy country where all the beasts speak like men. A nut tucked into the nest has tempted the squirrel close enough for the baby hawks to get a curious look at him.

This red fox expresses in a bored yawn his contempt for our cleverness as matched with his own. Or is this a laugh at the dogs he has outwitted? He uses every chance to evade them, and has a trick of getting behind them when they are on the hunt for him, and trotting in secure mockery at their heels.

Youth is playtime among animal folk as in human life, but in their rough and tumble these fox cubs are learning wit and quickness that will serve them well when they grow to be hunters and hunted.

The ears of a fox are keener even than his eyesight, and he depends on them more, both for news of his enemies abroad or for that rustle in the grass that might mean a field mouse or a woodchuck. Already this youngster is on the alert and pondering the rumors that come to his ears.

Fox cub and foxhound puppy, in the innocence of their youth, enjoy a happy companionship. Too soon the keen scent of the hound will be trained to run the fleet fox to its death. This is hunting not in accord with nature's law, for the fox dies not to feed the hunger of the hound, but for some vainglory that men call sport.

Who goes there?

The cottontail, by his telltale footprint. He must have vanished down one of his runways beneath the snow-laden bushes, in which he is often trapped by stalking weasel or goshawk. Or perhaps he is crouching close at hand, so motionless as to escape notice.

He who trains himself to read footprints in the snow has learned a new written language.

This baby rabbit has just opened its eyes upon the meadow world where it was born. The mother's soft and ever twitching nose seems to communicate reassurance.

Babyhood has the same appeal the world over. These little skunks, their eyes not yet opened, will never in later life seem so approachable. Skunks are domestic by nature; they lead a happy family life, going for walks all together in the evening air with the children tagging after their mother, and at night they make a furry heap of affection.

If a cat may look at a king, a skunk may look at a tortoise. This youngster's bright eye gives a hint of the intelligence and good nature of his kind. Save upon occasions when it uses its famous method of defense, it is free from all odor, and particularly neat and nice in its personal habits. This young skunk, certainly, is handsome enough to deserve the admiration of the tortoise.

The woodchuck is an easy-going fellow. All summer long he fattens himself on berries and green stuff, or perhaps on the pick of your vegetable garden, and when autumn winds turn bitter he will waddle down into his burrow under these rocks and sleep away hard times.

Bats make no home shelters, but simply hang themselves upside down to sleep the day through. The young, which are born in some cranny of barn or tree, often go with their mother on her night hunting, clinging about her neck. At dusk and before dawn bats are most active, sweeping the skies for insects.

This bright-eyed little Hamlet is not grieving for his Yorick. But curiosity calls a mouse's nose to inquire into any cranny, even, with a little persuasion, into the eyehole in the skull of a crow. Nature would make such a picture only by careless chance; it is man who might be inspired by it to a philosophic sonnet on life and death.

II

BIRDS ALL

In the airy world of the pine tops the black-throated green warbler makes a home for her children. Their lullaby is the wind through the shining needles, and a parent's song simple and drowsy as the midsummer hum of insects.

" Maids, maids, maids, put on your teakettle — ettle — ettle — ettle! " By this merry domestic melody you may know the song sparrow. The nest you will find in the bushes, oftenest near water, a neat little affair woven of grasses and frequently lined with horsehair.

To satisfy these clamorous young mouths with insects will keep the busy father and mother on the wing. But phœbes are devoted parents, as well as loyal mates and faithful friends, returning year after year to the same nesting sites.

This kingbird's nest was discovered in the crotch of a dead tree standing deep in spring waters. The camera was fastened to a branch and focused on the downy chicks, with a string tied to the shutter. Then the photographer, holding the other end of the string, waited concealed in a canoe beneath for just this moment of the mother bird's return, when the clicking shutter caught a tender glimpse of bird intimacy.

If there is a parable here for the young robin to learn, it may be that beauty is only skin deep, and that the grim-faced squat fellow to whom he has just been introduced is really a valued denizen of the garden.

All the happiness of home comes wistfully to mind at this glimpse of a blue-bird on its threshold in an old apple tree. No bird is closer to the human heart, neighbor as it is of our domestic joys and sorrows. Its sweet warble over the fields seems to be bringing back the spring, and when it leaves in late autumn, its farewell call comes to us with regret in it.

Her eggs secure beneath her cherishing breast, the mother wood thrush lifts her head to listen. Upon the late golden sunlight falls the serene benediction of her mate's song, that flute-like cadence which makes of the spring woods a temple.

The beautiful speedy arcs which the chimney swift cuts in the air are suggested by the composition of this photograph. It loves the twilights both of dawn and dusk, and you will see it then describing its winged geometry in flocks upon the dim air. Seldom will you see this unearthly bird alight, save in a hollow tree or in a chimney.

Knocked down by a falling brick in a storm, this nest full of newly hatched chimney swifts has been rescued from disaster. It is a curious bit of architecture, composed of twigs neatly interlaced rather as a basket is woven, and held together by a gum-like secretion from the stomach of the little builder.

The tree swallow, like the barn swallow, has a happy fancy for trimming its nest with feathers. It may build in a hollow tree or in a martin house or in the eaves of some deserted dwelling. Loving its kind, it dwells in flocks, which as they sail in circles overhead show clearly the white breasts that mark their kind.

Among the thickets the white-eyed vireo builds its pensile nest. It is a devoted and industrious parent, ever on the wing for insects and berries to provide its young. By nature vivacious and attentive, it warbles a varied melody, whimsically combining snatches from other bird-songs.

The vireo's white-rimmed eye, cocked upon the intruder, shows its vigilant and independent character. It is said that it will accost a loiterer near its graceful home with jerky syllables that seem to demand: "Who are you, eh?"

The crows are close to us in more than habitat. Their greed, their cleverness, audacity, and gabble should make them, of all birds, so comprehensible to man that he would make a truce with them. But perhaps we see our faults too plainly in them, and so — despite its usefulness in pest-control — the farmer levels his gun at the crow as at a hereditary enemy.

The nest of our American cuckoo is a jerry-built affair, a mere flooring of twigs through which the babies sometimes helplessly tumble. Not only is the mother bird a bad housekeeper and the nest often dirty, but she is an ineffective though devoted parent, hatching several broods a season but failing to raise all the young.

Four young flickers, nearly ready to fly, are taken from their nest in a hollow tree and given a preview of the world from the camera's vantage. The call of this woodpecker, like the whir of a watchman's rattle, and the flash of its golden-lined wings, make up a familiar part of summer's happiness.

The eggs, pale blue and beautifully scrawled in dark purple, of the red-winged blackbird are cradled in a nest among the reeds. In the windy spring weather the ringing whistle of the father bird sounds all around the marsh, and he is easy to see, marked as he is by brilliant scarlet epaulets that have given him the happy nickname of " soldier bird."

The nest of the killdeer is a casual affair, no more than a slight depression in the ground. Frequenting meadows near some waterside, it fills them with the sound of its windy plaint, forever restlessly taking wing, forever pursued, it seems, by some anxiety to which it must give tongue.

These young killdeer already show the handsome traits of their family. They will grow up to a life in the meadows and fields, hunting in the grasses, rising in a flock to wing away from real or fancied danger with their everlasting thin, sweet, querulous complaint: "*Killdee! Killdee!*"

Though you catch no more than a glimpse of it as it scrambles through the cattails, by its conspicuously white bill you will know it for a coot. The nest is built upon waters amid the screening herbage, but sometimes a wind blows it from its moorings and sends the brooding mother on an unexpected voyage over the marsh waters.

Deep in swamp grass lies the home of the Virginia rail. The eight eggs, with their creamy oval perfection patterned in ruddy brown, will become downy youngsters that grow into shy citizens of the fresh-water marshes.

The young of the Virginia rail are covered with jet-black down. Wherever they scamper, they are followed by the anxious attention of the mother bird, like chicks fussed over by a hen. Should this youngster venture too far amid the rushes, she will hear his thin peeping and come to be his comfort in a world still too big for him.

The Canada goose is a loyally domestic bird, and the gander stands ready to defend any attack on his nest with clamorous resentment. Yet they are mighty travelers too, and will set forth on a journey of thousands of miles straight as the arrowhead in which shape their flock is patterned, yet with no compass to guide them but the mysterious migratory impulse.

The goose, a symbol of absurdity upon the land, is in the elements of air and water a creature of power and beauty. It swims with strength and elegance, and is an agile diver, either to escape capture or to find itself a meal of succulent sedge roots. And when in a wedge-shape flock it passes high overhead with a clarion call, all of us who are bound to earth respond with a thrill of admiration.

The swan upon the water moves, a majestic figure of grace and peace. Despite the legend that gives it one last eloquent melody sung just before it dies, our common domestic swan is the most silent of birds, emitting nothing louder than a hiss.

The loon is at ease, not only upon the water, but under it. Apparently it can even make its toilet as it swims, preening its elegant black and white habit with nonchalance. A bird of the lonely lakes, it makes of any solitude a place more desolate, with its wild melancholy ringing scream.

The mallard duck is a devoted mother. If the young are hatched at any distance from the water, she carries them to it in her bill; at night she gathers her little flock under her wings. They are a lively crew, quick to learn how to swim and dive and catch insects, but their wings grow slowly and they cannot fly well before three months.

The awkwardness of youth is very touching. But these young green herons will grow into the grace of their tribe, which, when we see it in a figure solitary among the reeds and lilies of a pool, brings back the serenity of Oriental masterpieces.

This bald eagle took his own picture. The eel was bait, and from it a string led to the concealed camera. No photographer was at hand, but the eagle himself captured this glimpse of wild life at a Maine lake.

The Cooper's hawk is, for very good reasons, called the " chicken hawk " by farmers. He does more damage in the poultry yard than all other hawks combined. Birds, mammals, frogs, lizards, and insects are also on its diet list, but though it looks at this snake with greed mingled in its curiosity, the meal is too much to attempt.

When this boastful fledgling is grown, a bullfrog will not dare to face it with such contemptuous indifference. For the Cooper's hawk is a fierce and voracious hunter. It attacks wild birds as well as barnyard fowl; owls and crows will turn and fight it, and sometimes even the plucky though diminutive kingbird.

The nest of the Cooper's hawk is a well-built home, and the parents share the task of incubation. The young are bright and active, clad in pure white down. Already their eyes, which have seen so little of life, look upon it with a bold and predatory gaze.

So might the son of a robber chief stand and stare you down. He is losing the innocent whiteness of babyhood, beginning to be marked with the colors of his manhood. But the full perfection of adult plumage is not acquired for nearly three years.

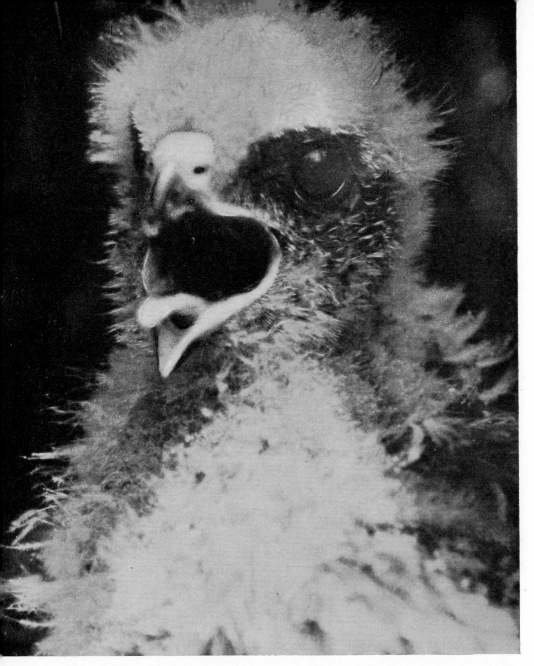

Kings are born to the crown, and artists to their genius. So a hawk is a predator from the egg forth, and even in downy babyhood its features show rapacity and boldness.

The whippoorwill is a bird of the night and the forest, oftener heard than seen. It nests upon the woodland floor, making no cradle for its eggs, but laying them simply upon the dry leaves it so much resembles. There they are hatched into fledglings almost indistinguishable from their background, which at an early age are able to run about after their parents.

The watchful eye of the brooding grouse shows her devotion and sagacity. The young can run about as soon as they are hatched; at a sign of danger they will squat upon the fallen leaves, while the mother, pretending lameness, flutters away along the ground to distract the attention of the hunter from her babies.

Our bobwhite is one of the country's most beloved citizens. Its brave and cheery nature, which ventures to face the winter out with us and to herald spring with a blithe whistle from some fence post, has deserved better of us than the bullets that have depleted its numbers.

The long bill of the woodcock is extremely sensitive, of more use to it in its search for insect food than are its curiously set eyes. Its wings are short and its flights make a whistling sound. For the most part it is a bird of the ground, and while upon the nest will sometimes tamely suffer even a stroking hand upon its back.

The barred owl is a valuable mouser and a bird to be respected for its sonorous utterance. If, when you are abroad at evening and hear its deep-toned query, you can answer with clever enough mimicry, you may succeed in drawing it forth from the shadows to find the intruding rival.

The screech owl is a hermit of the night. Discovered asleep at the bottom of its hole in an old apple tree, it has here been brought to the light, to blink a sleepy protest at the camera.

Nothing is drowsier than a screech owl by day, or more alert at night. Once those tufted ears had caught its scampering footfall, the mouse had little chance to escape. Nature, which makes no place for pity, keeps its balance by a great rough justice of its own.

The snowy owl is a bird of the northern solitudes. Swift of flight, silent as the driving flakes, it darts upon its prey with those relentless talons which alone of its body are free from the close warm covering of plumage that covers even its nostrils.

An English sparrow resting in a brier bush makes against gray autumnal skies a picture serene as an ancient Oriental drawing upon silk and proves once more that in nature rarity is no criterion of worth.

III

COOL—BLOODED ONES

The sphere of the amphibians is divided between water and land. Born to the water, they climb out of it as they develop, returning to lay their eggs in that maternal medium.

The chill embrace of the frogs in the spring pond will later provide a supply of wriggling tadpoles to feed the ravening hunger of the under-water world. The eggs are fertilized by the male after they are laid, in the manner of the fishes.

Black pearls of life, the frog's eggs lie embedded in translucent jelly. Under the warming sun of springtime the tiny tadpoles will develop and wriggle free at last.

Gradually the tail of the tadpole is absorbed, and the wriggler of the waters becomes the leaper of the land. Here are shown three stages in the process of a frog's development; the species, however, differ.

Even as the frog is mirrored in the pond, so its life history reflects the course of animal evolution. Beginning as a tadpole, with gills and a fish-like circulation, it is transformed in time to an air-breathing denizen of the land.

From an ancient and watery past once shared by the ancestors of now proud mammals, the frog looks back at us with a saturnine smile, as one who knows that we are all cousins under the skin.

This has the appearance of a debate on the old subject of whether it is better to be a big frog in a little puddle or a little frog in a big puddle. Nature leaves no room for argument; she made the fellow on the right a leopard frog, and created his fellow a bullfrog — recognizable by the fact that his eardrums are so much larger than his eyes.

The green frog, here devouring a newt, is very much a fellow of the waters. As a tadpole, it passes the winter under the ice, emerging late in spring in mature form — with, apparently, a ferocious appetite.

The toes of the tree frog are adapted to clinging and climbing, and it is further specialized in its ability to alter its coloring to conform to its background.

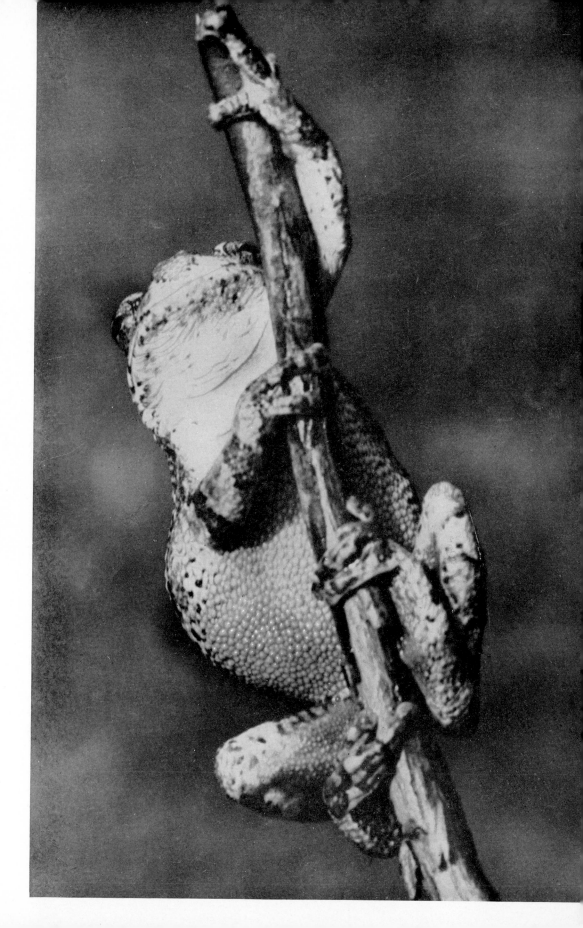

" When the three-toed
Tree toad
Sings his sweet ode
To the moon — "
spring, the time of idyls, has arrived.

The toad is an animal chiefly of the land, but its eggs are laid in the waters, in stringy masses. For the rest, it is a dusty creature; some water it must have, however, and its method of drinking is through its skin.

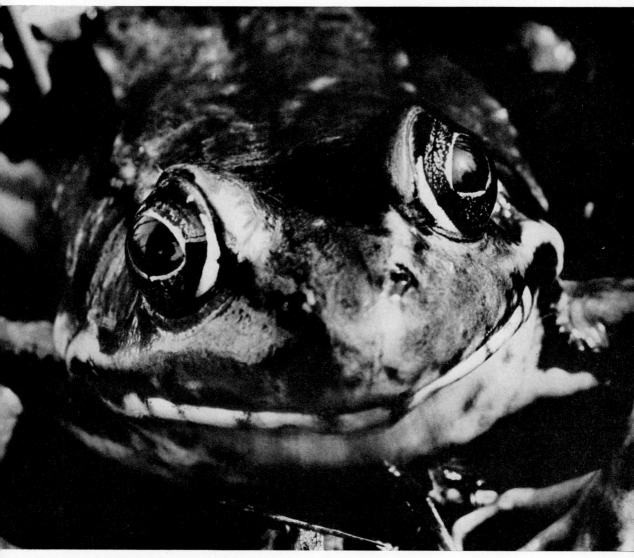

This frog's smile is so engaging that it takes a moment before one observes reflected in one of its eyes the reedy margin of the pond where the sun is setting, and in the other a glimpse of the crouching photographer.

This benignant citizen of the garden usefully devours insect pests. His dry warty skin is like that of his toadstool parasols in appearance — but they are not so innocent as he, for they are amanitas and may be fatally poisonous.

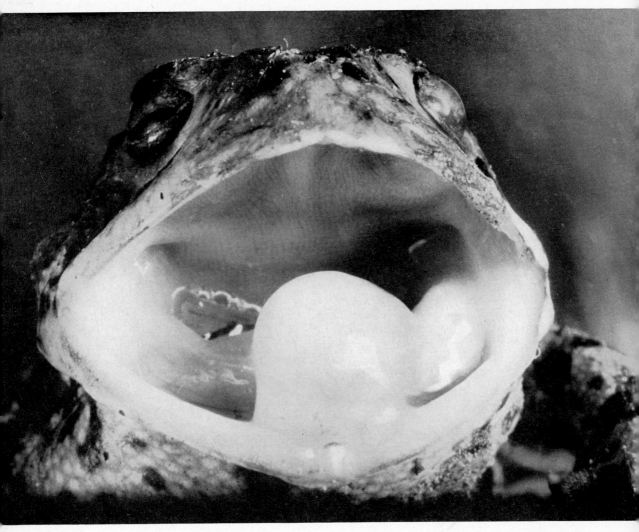

The tongue of a toad is attached at the front of the mouth and is split at the end. Like forked lightning it flashes forth to seize an insect on its sticky surface.

Only the ignorant fear the toad and the golden garden spider. Both are friendly neighbors to us, keeping down the insects with which man sustains a pitched battle over our common environment. The toad will not give you warts, nor the spider any dangerous bite; she asks only to be let alone over the important business of her egg case.

Fancy makes friends of a toad and a tortoise where sunlight through the uncurling ferns creates a fairy-tale out of nature.

His throat distended with the tender passion, the toad trills his ode to some listening mate. From the clear shrilling of the spring peepers to the plucked cello note of the green frog, it sings one song and tells one story — that the cold heart of winter is broken, and buds are swelling on the willows around the marsh.

Some snakes give birth to young, and some lay eggs. These snake babies are emerging into a world filled with prejudice against them and superstitions about them. A little familiarity with the subject of snakes will discover many more fascinating facts about them than there are absurd legends.

Coiled like a steel spring to strike, this ribbon snake makes an exquisite design. Nor is there anything to fear from him; the dart of his tiny tongue is harmless, but it probably helps him to understand his environment, for the vision and hearing of a snake are poor, while the tongue is extremely sensitive.

The garter snake, securing himself by the tail, is free to thrust. The direct and angular spread of the branches together with the animal's sinuous fluidity make a lovely composition.

Newts are amphibians, some living on land and some preferring water. They are graceful and agile little creatures; try to catch one along the brook, and very likely all you will get for your pains is a glimpse of vermilion spots vanishing beneath the ripples.

" *Newts and blind-worms, do no wrong . . .*
Beetles black, approach not near! "
Thus sang Shakespeare's fairies when their Queen lay down to sleep.

The slug loves the night and the dampness. Its eggs are laid in the soil, under stones, or in decaying wood. It is, generally speaking, a snail without a shell; where it has passed in wood or garden you will find a faint silvery track.

The newly hatched brook trout still carries with it part of the yolk sac which provides nourishment as the little fish grows. Manifold are the ways in which nature feeds her growing babies; in progressively higher stages of animal life the period of infancy is proportionately longer.

The snapping turtle is an amphibian at home on land or water. However, if
it does not care to be " at home " to anybody at all, it has but to withdraw
completely into its shell, and the intruder may knock in vain.

A fierce pride in the days when the world belonged to his forebears, armored reptilian giants with all the traits he carries on, gleams in the eyes of the tortoise. Now only the shrunken pond in the summer woods is left him to rule, but there he swims and dives and suns himself on a log in lethargic contentment with his fallen estate.

The turtle lays its eggs upon the land, but as soon as the young hatch, they migrate to water.

To see only what is pretty in nature is to be purblind. The salamander and the skunk cabbage make a composition that speaks to us eloquently of the earliest wet sweet beginning of spring, and of the world's long-ago spring too, when all of earth was a marsh, and life still crawled in the velvet mud.

IV

MONSTROUS AND MYSTERIOUS

The world of the insects is one beneath our feet, too often beneath our notice. Yet insects alone rival man in the conquest of the earth today, successfully occupying all environments except the sea, and making use of the very materials on which we rely. This coquetry of grasshoppers between toadstools is an elfin picture, but in reality the insect world is one of terrible hungers, monstrous habits, and mysterious compulsions.

Summer has come when the May beetle, or June bug, begins to bang against the screen door. Its incessant attacks show how hard is the armor of chitin it wears over its wings, and yet the filmy wings themselves are made of this same substance — the stuff of which all the insect world is created.

The long-horned beetle is a creature of impressive dignity. As a grub and chrysalis it passes an extraordinarily long youth in the cells and tunnels it bores within an oak or pine tree. Before it emerges as this magnificent beetle, twenty years may have gone by.

Minute and monstrous, our rivals the insects share our world, and only the camera with its magnifying lens shows us their features plain. The glittering beetle crawling up the acorn sees with another gaze than ours the furry moth that stares him down with complex eyes.

First and second violin in summer's orchestra, the grasshopper and the katydid are here posed together on an apple for bandstand. The full sphere of the fruit, the jutting angles of the insect legs, again remind us, by the boldness of the composition, how much strange beauty lies unheeded about us.

This solitary wasp has built a mud nest in which to lay her eggs and is busily storing it with spiders for the future provision of her young. Each spider is paralyzed by a well-placed stab of the wasp's poisonous sting, so that the meat, sealed up in the nest, will remain fresh for the wasp larvæ when they shall have hatched.

How ants communicate with one another is still unfathomed by the mind of man. Certain it is that they exchange messages; friends are recognized, strangers known at once.

The wings are worn only at the nuptial season; when the wedding is over, the queen descends to earth, tears off her wings, and retires from the light to her manifold duties.

The carpenter ant tunnels for his tribe a labyrinthine home. The social life of ants is, almost alone among insect ways, comparable to mankind's for its complexity and elaborate development. But while we struggle to meet our problems with intelligence, the rule of ant civilization is by instinct, a giant master-mind instinct of the tribe itself, which issues imperative commands to each individual.

Sudden disaster to the ant colony, as when curious fingers strip away the bark of a log in which it has tunneled a home, brings every member into instant action. The future of the race lies in the passive bundles that are the pupæ. So the most immediate necessity to the alert defenders of the ant common-weal is to carry the babies away to safety.

Aphids, commonly called " ant cows," are plant lice which exude a sweetish substance much relished by certain species of ants, which take pains to rear and nurture their tiny " cattle."

The industry and ambition of the ant are indomitable. The ant here posed with a robber fly is quite capable of dragging it away to the nest; it has been calculated that if an ant were as big as a man it could pull over two hundred thousand pounds.

This interior of a bumblebee's nest, formed perhaps in some old burrow of a field mouse, shows a social life of which the queen is ruler and mother. She lays and incubates the eggs, feeds the larvæ upon the pollen and honey she has gathered and stored, and broods upon the cocoons which they spin about themselves. From these the first daughter bees emerge to help her with her household tasks.

The bumblebee emerges, handsome in black and gold velvet. With her brushy legs and back she gathers pollen, and with her tongue she rifles the flowers of their nectar. Hers is the work of a summer only; unlike the hive of the honeybee, the bumblebee's nest is merely an annual home.

A bee at its rites among apple blossoms shows the most marvelous partnership in nature. Amply repaid by the flower's golden hoard of pollen and nectar, the bee performs its invaluable role in the great work of cross-pollination.

The gray paper house of the wasp is made of well-chewed wood. The queen mother begins its building, laying in it, as she builds, the eggs that will become the future communistic colony. The house, which is composed of tiers of flat paper combs enclosed in walls of waterproof paper, gradually grows in size under the industrious attentions of the wasp workers.

The wasp is able to enter the narrow doors and penetrate the halls of its paper home by means of a neat folding of its wings into three pleats. The nest is heated by the warmth of the many wasp bodies, and insulated by air spaces between the walls.

Not only the materials for her house but all the food her babies eat must be chewed up by the queen mother. The worker wasps are forever occupied with repairs on the home castle, all done by the jaws, with the use of saliva.

Magnified by the lens, the sting of a hornet appears a fearful weapon, a broad blade with barbs nicked in it. Moreover, into the wound as it makes it the wasp ejects a fluid that feels like liquid fire in our flesh.

Terrifying in his white robber-mask, the bald-faced hornet faces us down. Few will stay to argue with him. But it is believed that it is our own alarm at him that prompts his sting, possibly because fear may give out an actual odor which warns or irritates him.

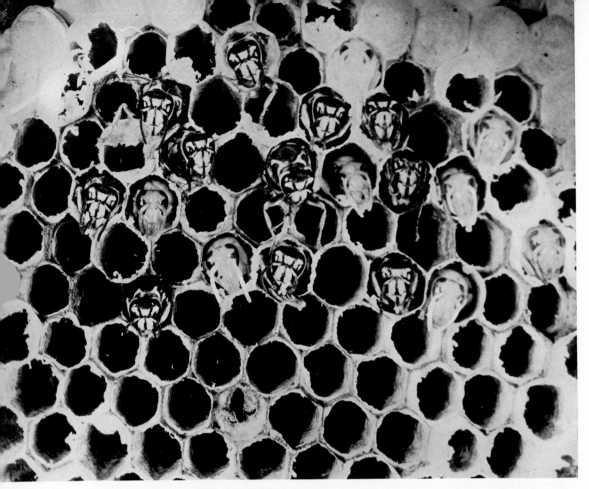

No human skill in engineering could improve upon the principle of the six-sided cells which make up the gray paper castles of the wasps and hornets. Though individual will and intelligence seem, on the whole, to be denied the insects, the commands of their instinct are exact and irresistible.

When the fiddles of the crickets strike up in the fields, we know that corn is ripe and summer at its apogee. For the most part, the insect world is a place of monstrous strangeness to mankind, but the cricket is a little creature of sympathetic and homelike associations for us, and can even be made a pet.

In China and Japan the cricket has for long centuries been a favorite, for its cheerful disposition, its fiddling, and its prowess in battle. In the serene Orient of the past, fighting crickets were matched in bouts together, singing crickets kept in little golden cages to make music for the ladies of the court.

The cricket is greedy in appetite and catholic in taste. It will eat anything from flesh to cloth, having sharp enough mouth parts to bite through the toughest fiber. It is probable that through its delicate antennæ it receives a thousand scents and promises far too faint for our gross human senses to perceive.

The robber fly is a ruthless pirate of the airways. With its huge compound eyes, containing as many as four thousand lenses, it can detect even a passing gnat.

The praying mantis, inoffensive to man, is nevertheless a creature of ravening ferocity. The death-blow struck by its bladed forearms is faster than the eye can follow. As mating rites are concluded, the female begins to devour the male. And these traits are rendered more horrifying to our eyes by the fact that the mantis, almost uniquely among insects, can turn its head about like a man and thus present to us a little countenance uncannily malevolent.

Mantis and butterfly have been posed under magnification for a moment's
unlikely truce. Thus are revealed to us the odd little jointed head of the
mantis and its huge deadly forearms, folded with an appearance of piety;
opposite, the butterfly wears an air of apparent naïveté. But these attributes
of hypocrisy and innocence which we give to the insects are all in the human
eye. Nature does not judge her other creatures by our standards.

The mantis builds her nest of a frothy excretion from her body which hardens with exposure to the air. As she makes it, she lays her eggs in it; the task takes her about two hours. The young are hatched in fully adult form, unlike the higher types of insect which proceed through the stages of egg, larva, and mature insect, for the mantis belongs to one of the most primitive families on earth.

Before the dragonfly is free to spangle the blue summer day with its darting speed, it must pass a year or more in the pond waters as a nymph. In this form it is a stealthy and tigerish creature, preying upon all the smaller denizens of the pond, even the tadpoles. Here is shown, under high magnification, the under lip, ending in pincers which it shoots out, to grip its prey and pull it back into a ravening maw.

When the dragonfly's term of life under the water is ended, it crawls above the surface, on some reed perhaps, and there goes through its translation. The chitinous shard of the nymph splits down the back, and the winged insect begins its struggle to emerge.

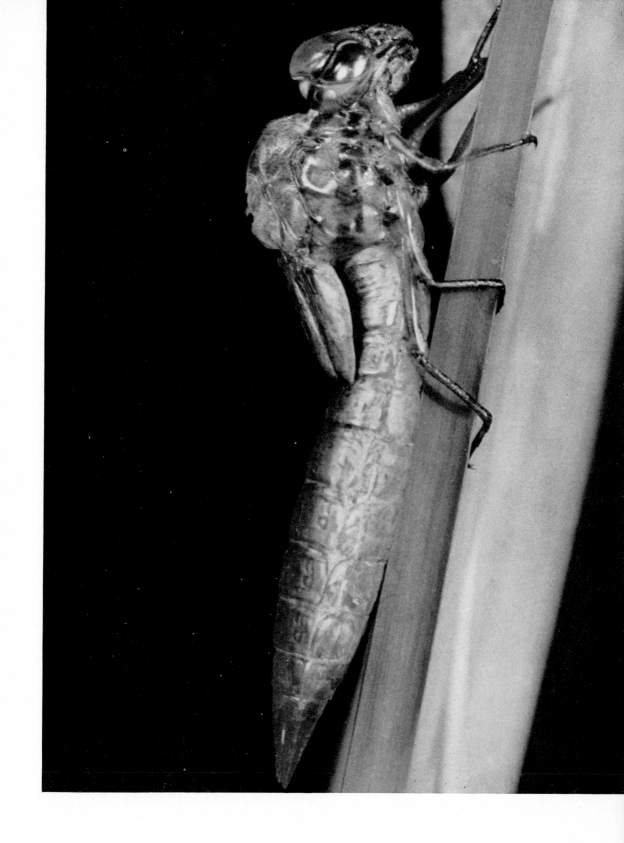

Wrenching itself outward and upward, the damp and crumpled insect rears toward the light of day. It faces now an existence totally different from that of its previous incarnation.

The dragonfly can dart like a thread of light through the summer airs at a speed of nearly a mile a minute. Here that bullet flight has ended in tragedy, as the golden garden spider approaches to make complete its capture.

Escaped from another and darker life, freed from a form outgrown, the triumphant insect clings damp and weak, breathing in the unfamiliar air of summer. Beneath it remains the shell of its past, a thing without life or further purpose.

Here are shown three stages of the dragonfly's progress — the discarded nymph case, the newly emerged insect, not yet hardened or strengthened enough for flight, and the final stage in which it has spread its glittering wings, ready to take off upon the swift adventure of aerial life.

As the water-lily belongs to one of the most primitive of flower families, so is the dragonfly a descendant of some of the earliest insects. In the dank fern-tree jungles of the Carboniferous Age there flitted dragonflies with a wing-spread of thirty inches!

The wing of a dragonfly is supported by a complex network of veins, containing several thousand separate cells. In its iridescent translucence, it brings to mind the beauty of a cathedral's stained-glass window.

Hugely magnified, the head of a cicada nymph reveals the features of a clumsily armored denizen of the underworld. One species passes seventeen years in the earth, arising into the light for the week or so of aerial existence that culminates its strange history.

The dog days are here when the drone of the cicada sounds above the summer hum. It passes its youth underground, feeding upon the juices of roots, then crawls to the light, splits down the back, and liberates the adult form. Here are shown the empty shell of the nymph, and the newly freed mature insect.

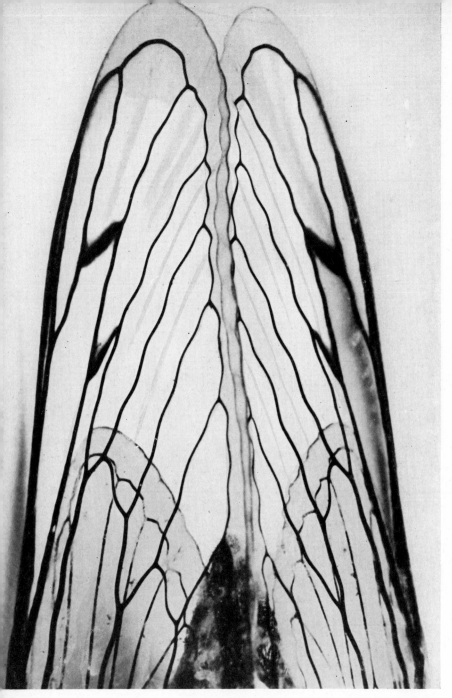

Beneath the wing of a cicada, chitin-spun, exquisitely patterned, lies the musical instrument of the insect, a drum-skin which is vibrated to produce the soaring monotone that makes the August skies seem so blue, the ripening fields so golden.

In this simple and everyday composition are displayed the two kinds of symmetry in which nature is largely patterned. The butterfly is an example of bilateral, or two-sided, symmetry, while the symmetry of the button-bush flower is the other fundamental sort, the radial.

The "lady-bug" upon the sparrow's egg makes a quiet declaration of both the form and the pattern which, in infinite variation, compose the beauty of nature. This pretty little beetle got her popular name in the Middle Ages, when, quaintly enough, she was dedicated to the Virgin, and her tribe became the "beetles of Our Lady."

The earwig is an immigrant upon our shores from Europe, where folklore gave it the absurd reputation of burrowing into the ear of a sleeper and thence into his brain. The forceps in which its body ends are probably weapons, since it raises them when threatened.

An insect colloquy is carried on in terms beyond us. On the left is a rove beetle, a quite harmless scavenger. Confronting him, a grasshopper inquires of him with twiddling antennæ.

The katydid is a creature of Titania's realm, clad as it is in pale-green gauze. The male is the most persistent of fiddlers, scraping away with a file on his left wing over a ridge on his right — a familiar music on Midsummer's Eve.

Not only does the katydid hear with its legs, but it can jump with them a hundred times its length. Thus it has sprung to the swaying balcony of a Turk's-cap lily, from which vantage point it can turn its many-faceted eye upon whatever drama takes place in the wood tonight.

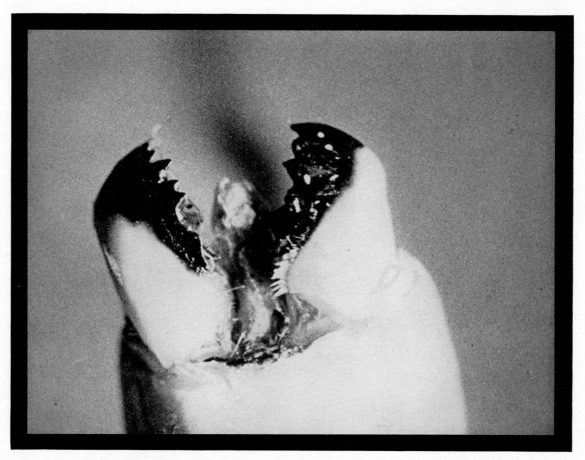

These jaws belong to that elfin little bore, the katydid. They will feed it only for a season. This is an ephemeral creature, which will pass with the summer's passing, when the first cruel frost stiffens the grasses.

The equine countenance of the katydid is an amiable one, when you get a fairy's-eye view of it. But however closely you scan this grotesque head, you will not find the creature's ears. It happens to carry them, instead, in its knees!

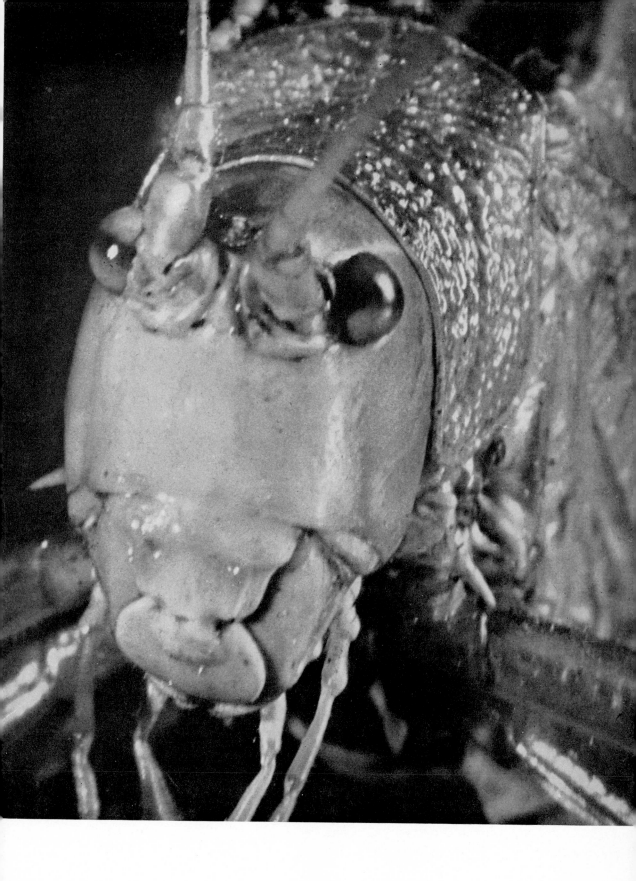

Fellow travelers of the summer air pause to inquire of one another upon their way. The silverspotted butterfly on the left is facing a monarch, one of our commonest and most handsome species, which owes much of its success to the fact that in both the caterpillar and the adult stage it is distasteful to birds.

It is the scales upon the wing of a butterfly that give it its exquisite color and iridescence. Magnification here shows what a gauzy texture can be spun of chitin, the same stuff that makes the horn of the beetle or the sting of the wasp.

The eye of a butterfly is, proportionately, enormous, and composed of thousands of facets. Yet the insect is a short-sighted creature, for though the eye reflects distant objects, the brain seems unable to deal with any much farther than ten feet away.

The monarch butterfly has an affinity with milkweed. This plant alone is the food of its gorging caterpillar. And when autumn comes and the milkweed pods burst open to let the downy seeds adrift upon the last warm airs, the monarch butterflies also set forth, in companionable clouds, upon a drifting and mysterious migration to the south.

Passing his brief life in fair weather and supping flittingly on the nectar of flowers, the butterfly seems rather a lightweight and frivolous creature. But the male is a bold-hearted and pugnacious fighter, doing battle to win his mate and fiercely driving off the young butterfly bloods that may hang about his lady.

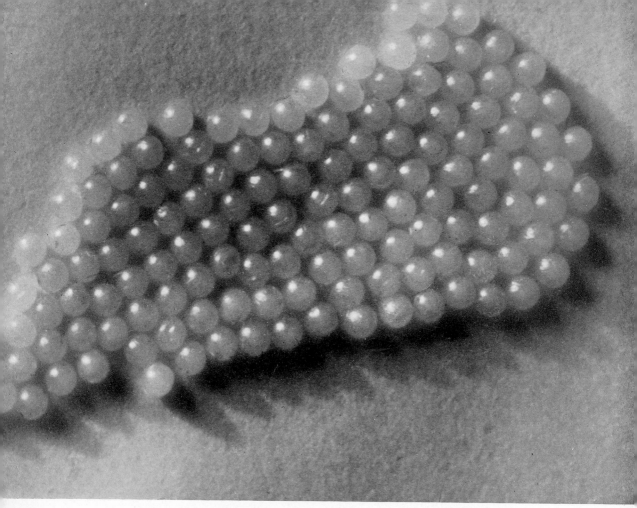

Under high magnification, the eggs of the swallowtail butterfly appear luminous as pearls, each shining sphere a gem precious with future life.

The caterpillar of the black swallowtail has just attached its tail to a twig and spun a strong line of silk about its body to support it while it begins the making of its chrysalis.

A tiger swallowtail upon wide-open roses seems to us a culmination in life's purpose. But what that may be, no man can say; it is enough that in its infinite experimentation life has given us the by-product of beauty.

Within the chrysalis, withdrawn and secret, the pupa has been preparing for this moment of emergence, transformed into a butterfly. With patient punctuality nature repeats this miracle over and over with every season, and yet the mystery remains, the uplifting sense of destiny about us greater than our comprehension.

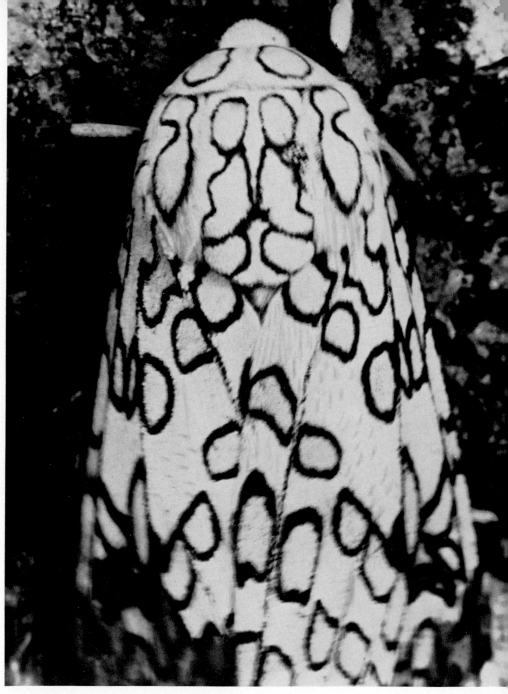

The moth is a creature of the dusk and night, wrapped in soft folds, having often feathery antennæ. Butterflies, which love the sun, hold their wings erect with sprightly grace, and their antennæ are club-shaped. The moths are the more numerous but the less observed, since they love the hours when the earth rolls out of sunshine.

June is the month for the first roses and for the emergence and mating of our largest moths. The dew on the petal, the bloom on the wing, are life at its freshest and most immaculate.

The stages in the life of butterfly or moth, from the earth-crawling grub, through the death-in-life trance of the cocoon, to the final free emergence of the winged thing, have long struck the human mind as a miraculous progress. But the life of the winged form is short, and less important, in nature's economy, than that of the larval stage, and for anyone with an unprejudiced viewpoint this striped and undulant caterpillar has a tigerish beauty all its own.

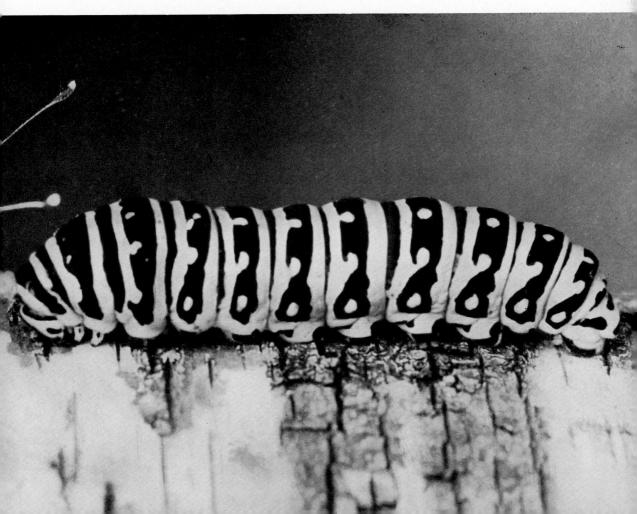

The fairy-like sphinx moth may often be seen as a winged blur supping nectar from the flowers in your garden at dusk.

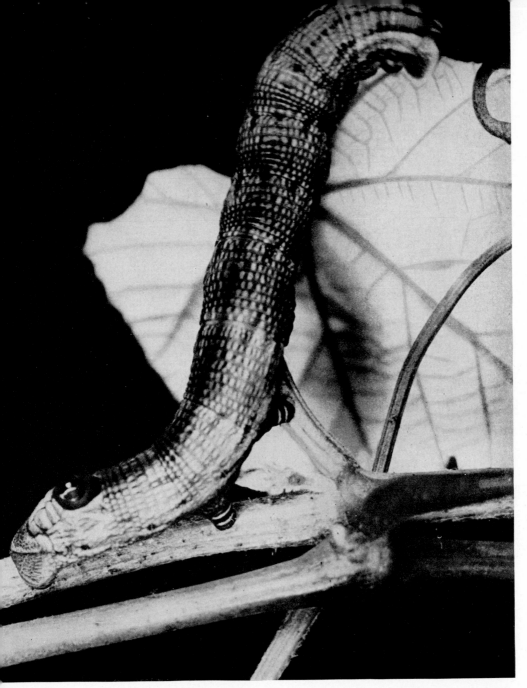

The caterpillar of the sphinx moth is an incredible affair, having in its tail a tubercle amazingly like an eye in appearance, which is said by some to frighten off the birds which might find the creature a juicy tidbit.

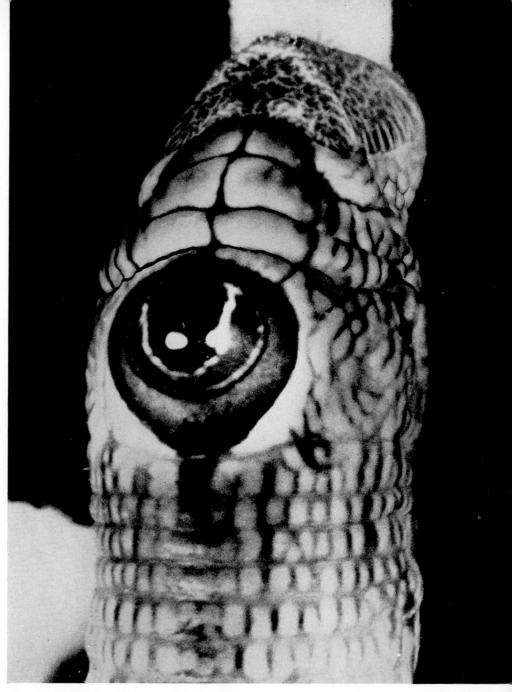

Close up, the lifelike " eye " in the tail of the sphinx-moth caterpillar seems to give us a baleful glance. Moreover, scientists have reported that this caterpillar is capable of emitting a squeak!

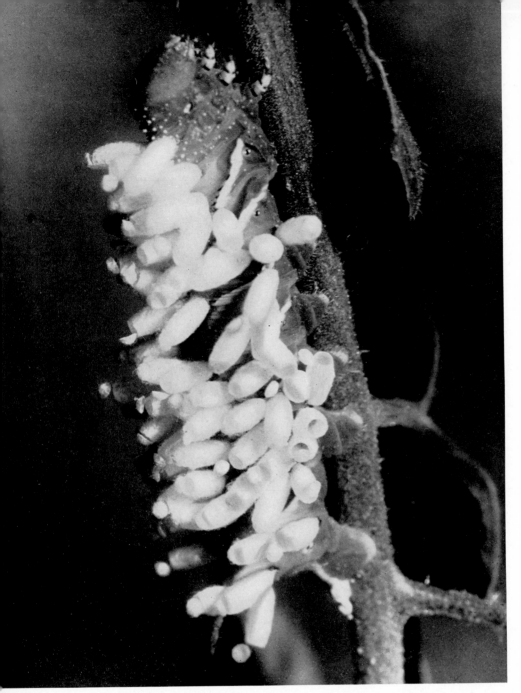

The ichneumon fly is a deadly foe of the caterpillar. Its grubs are parasitic, feasting and even pupating upon their living host.

Shortly after the Civil War an amateur entomologist in Massachusetts was experimenting with a moth imported from Europe. It escaped from control and became one of our chief insect public enemies — the dreaded gypsy moth.

These are the features of a criminal at large who is " Wanted! " If you should happen to capture what you think is a gypsy moth, you should send the specimen, with a report, to your state entomologist, or to the U. S. Bureau of Entomology at Washington.

Millions of dollars have been spent to fight the ravages of the gypsy moth. It has not been possible to exterminate it, but its destructive energies have been controlled to some extent. Here is a specimen that has just gone into the chrysalis stage.

The beautiful plume-like antennæ of the moth are the seat of extraordinarily acute senses. In the males of some species they can detect the presence of a female at a great distance, even if she is enclosed in a house and surrounded with innumerable other stronger odors.

Insect portraiture reveals the dazzling complexity of detail in nature that escapes our unaided vision. To the left is a crane fly, often mistaken for a giant mosquito, but it does not bite. The hawk moth on the right displays its exquisitely coiled long tongue, adapted to supping nectar from any long-throated corolla.

The tomato caterpillar is the larval stage of the hawk moth. The next stage is pupation, shown here, which takes place in or on the ground. The "handle" of the chrysalis is a sheath for the long tongue.

Atop a cattail are posed a robber fly and a hawk moth. Insect photography can be a sport as exciting as big-game stalking, and even a city back yard will prove a jungle full of strange monsters.

That the outspread spotted wings of this moth, held with the antennæ downward, so much resemble an owlish face only goes to show how warped may be much of our human view of things. Nature is not patterned according to the accumulated prejudices and preferences of mankind, and only by laying these aside and searching for uncolored fact do we ever come to understand her in any degree truly.

Unblemished, palpitant, this beautiful Cecropia moth has just emerged from its cocoon — a transfiguration that from time immemorial has filled the human mind with a sense of radiant promise.

There are over eight thousand species of moths to be found in America, but few to view with the velvet beauty of the Promethea, spreading its wings in unconscious pride upon the still uncurling fronds of a cinnamon fern.

The newly emerged Cecropia appears the ultimate triumph of its strange life history, toward which the crawling grub and moveless chrysalis were but lowly steps. Yet in this final form the insect is unable even to eat, having poorly developed and apparently functionless mouth parts. In this phase it but mates and starts the cycle over again, and only our human love of beauty determines that the winged stage is the crowning one.

The giant water bug must be to the inhabitants of the fresh-water world an appalling monster. When full grown, it may measure more than two inches in length, and even little fishes have reason to turn tail and flee from it. Not all its life is passed under water; it flies from pond to pond, usually at night, and may be seen banging in helpless fascination about a street light.

The water scorpion is an eerie little citizen of the brook. There is no sting in its tail, which is rather an air-pipe through which it breathes, resting below the surface with no more than the tip exposed. Lurking thus stealthily, it snatches a passing victim in its long forearms and stalks away to devour it at leisure.

The serene surface of a pond hides a thronging world of driving appetites and fleeing fears. This pretty little newt could not escape the tiger of the bottoms, the giant water bug. Hunger is the master law of nature, and pity has no place in it.

The Dytiscus beetle is a bold and handsome diver of the ponds, with the voracious courage required in the life below the surface. Its larval form is equally predacious and has earned it the name of water tiger. Here a leech has fallen victim to the adult beetle.

The caddice-worms build themselves little houses snug about their bodies, fastening themselves securely into them at the tail end. These curious composite habitations may be made of bits of leaf, twigs, pebbles, or snail shells and lined with a sort of silk fiber.

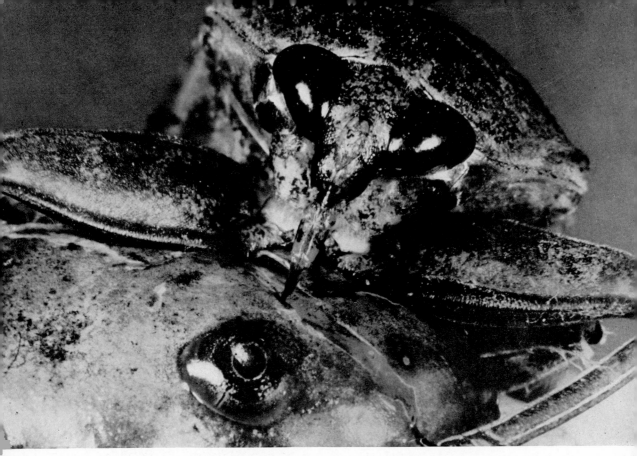

To see the world about us clear, we must sweep horror from our eyes, and understand that the giant water bug here thrusting the death-stroke into the head of a tadpole to suck its blood knows neither good nor evil but only the laws of its kind.

The insect people have, all of them, just six legs, so that the spider, having eight legs, is not one of them. But she too is one of the mysteriously wise, the tinily fierce, who share our world, all but unheeded, yet prospering mightily on their lowly plane.

The body of a spider is built in two parts, not three like an insect's. The fore part of the body carries the head and four pairs of legs; the lower half is large and contains the spinning machine. The eyes are usually eight, and they are simple, not compound.

The orb web of a spider, picked out with dewdrops glittering in the morning light, is invariably built in the same methodical manner. It is composed of smooth, tough silk strands and of others which are sticky and thus constitute the real snare. The spider carefully oils her legs before she begins work on these sticky threads, to avoid getting entangled herself.

Our handsome golden garden spider always signs her masterpiece with a bold zigzag band of silk.

Here, under high magnification, are displayed the spinnerets of the spider, which move with the dexterity of short blunt fingers to make the steel-strong, lacy fabric of the web. As the liquid silk is ejected through them, it hardens at the touch of air, and the little master craftsman is able to vary it in quality and quantity according to her needs.

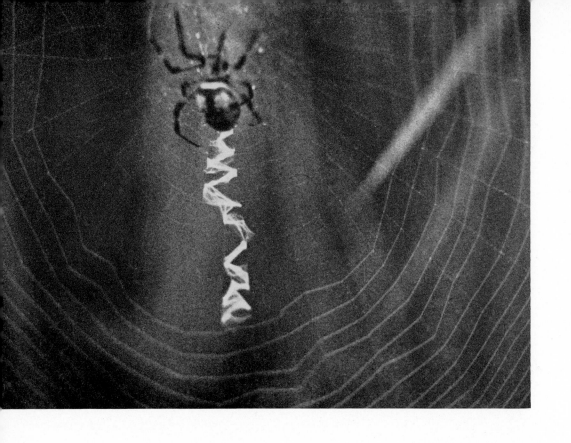

Often a " telegraph line " in the net warns the spider by its vibration that a victim has arrived. Then she will rush out to complete the capture, sometimes, if the victim is large like this grasshopper, shaking the net further to entangle it. Then she begins to prepare its shroud.

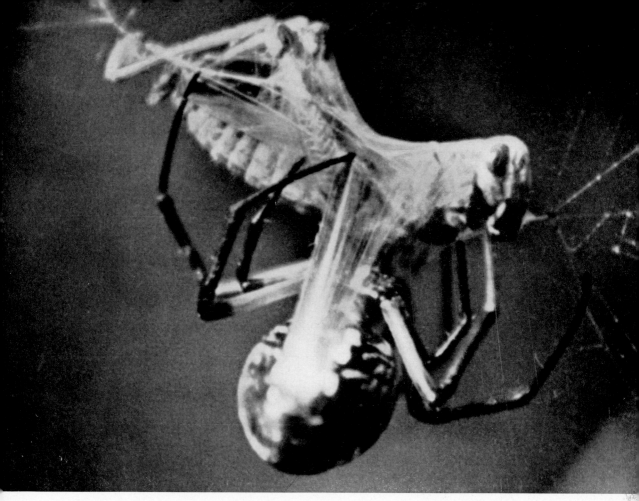

When the grasshopper is helplessly bound in silken wrappings, the spider will plunge her fangs into it, injecting poison, and then at her leisure suck its juices. Fierce as she is to the insect world, the spider is an ally of man, helping to keep down all manner of pests.

In a close-up, the spider's fierce fangs are intimidating enough. Yet though all spiders are poisonous to their insect victims, none in the United States are really dangerous to human beings save the black widow, easily recognized by her show-button body with its red hour-glass marking.

The orb-weaving spiders, with their large abdomens often patterned in gold and black, are handsome jewels of the garden. Here is one beside an egg sac. She can lay as many as a thousand eggs at a time.

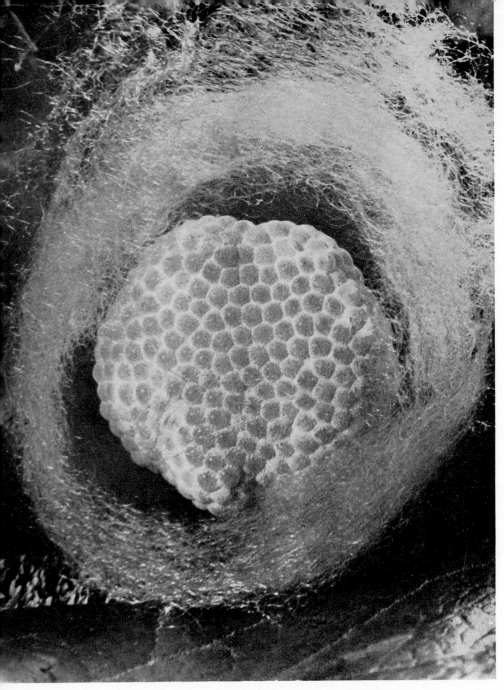

Here the egg sac has been cut open, to show the strong soft walls and the seeds of life stored within.

Baby spiders, hundreds of them, burst astonished upon the world. The young of many species are parachute explorers. When autumn comes, they climb to some little heights and spin out into the breeze a line of silk; on this they sail away to see the world and spread the spider population.

The spider and the fly are here shown under high magnification in the final act of their tragedy. The paralyzing fangs are sinking in, and soon the fly's vital juices will be part of the spider's ability and cunning.

Not all spiders are web-builders. The wolf spider catches her prey in the chase and carries her precious egg sac with her wherever she goes.

Women have things their own way in the spider world. They are the spin-
ners and the masters of the web. They are much larger than the males — in
one species the female is one hundred times larger than her mate — and frequently the wedding ends in a cannibal feast by the bride upon the groom.

Fierce maternal jealousy is expressed in the grip of this diving spider upon her bundle of future babies. When the time comes, she will rip the sac open and let them out into life.

A Note on the Type

The text of this book is set in Caledonia, a new Linotype face designed by W. A. Dwiggins. Caledonia belongs to the family of printing types called " modern face " by printers — a term used to mark the change in style of type-letters that occurred about 1800. Caledonia is in the general neighborhood of Scotch Modern in design, but is more freely drawn than that letter.

The book was composed, printed, and bound by The Plimpton Press, Norwood, Massachusetts. The paper was made by S. D. Warren Company, Boston. The illustrations were reproduced by half-tone engravings made by Eagle Photo-engraving Company, New York.